A collection of stories from the past,
Including the Senior Ministry Years

Growing Up in Brooklyn, New York

SAMUEL AQUILA &
ROSEANN AQUILA SPAULDING

A collection of stories from the past
Including the Senior Ministry Years

Growing Up in Brooklyn, New York

SAMUEL AQUILA

&

ROSEANN AQUILA SPAULDING

ISBN: 978-1-64184-660-8

Dedication

Sam

This book is dedicated to my wife, Filomena; my son,
Ralph; my daughters Susan and Ruth; and to my family.
The many hours dedicated to school, travel, and work
left me unable to spend adequate time with my family.
I want to let my wife, Filomena—and the whole world—know
how much I love them, and how much I desire and plan
to spend more time with them, having a closer
relationship and having fun.

Roseann

Timmy, my love…
Your belief in my ability to forge ahead on such an
unfamiliar road, got me through many long nights that
rolled into early mornings. Thank you for believing in
my vision for this project, your encouragement and
generosity made this book a reality, twice.
For my children and grandchildren this is your legacy;
a heritage of prayerful family, who intimately knew
God and invited the Holy Spirit into their lives.

Acknowledgements

I would like to thank my niece, Roseann; my wife,
Filomena; and my family for encouraging me
to write this collection of short stories:
"Growing Up in Brooklyn, New York."

Preface

I was always fascinated by my Uncle Sammy and Aunt Phyllis. I cannot remember an occasion when I was not excited to spend time with them. Over the years, Uncle Sammy would entertain us with astonishing magic tricks—the Mickey Mouse ring trick, static electricity pencil, vanishing coin, and, my personal favorite, the disappearing finger—I am still looking for mine.

My aunt and uncle were in possession of one of my favorite dogs, a German Shepherd named King. They had a lovely yard that backed up to a wooded forest. It was the kind of place where nature beckoned to be ventured and discovered, and I enjoyed many adventures there with my cousins and King.

One of the many gifts my aunt had, was the ability to turn ordinary pancakes into a food that greeted you with a smile. Aunt Phyllis and Uncle Sammy had three lovely children, all of whom I hold dear to my heart—and with some of whom I have had a few noteworthy escapades.

Filomena or Aunt Phyllis, as we affectionately call her, designed and crafted her own enchanting princess-style wedding dress. She is truly a masterful seamstress. I believe Kate Middleton, the Duchess of Cambridge, had replicated part of my aunt's wedding dress for her wedding. I remember when my daughter Haleigh was in eighth grade, she had a presidential ball project and was in need of a dress to complete the project. Aunt Phyllis graciously made her an exact replica of an Oleg Cassini ivory silk gazar dress with matching shawl—just like Jacqueline Kennedy wore for a dinner in Venezuela. I believe we still have that little number.

Samuel Aquila was a soil engineer, but he worked many years to become a mechanical engineer—managing a family, a job by day, and school at night. Uncle Sammy attributes his ability to construct and figure out nearly impossible situations, to seeking the wisdom of the Lord and to God bestowing upon him the solutions and creativity to move forward. He helped engineer Apollos 5-12, during which Uncle Sammy had meetings with Neil Armstrong and fellow astronauts. They conversed about the mechanics and inner workings of the projects that lay before them. The intelligence of my Uncle Sammy astonishes me, even to this day.

Just a few days ago, we were having a conversation regarding the measure of gravity on the moon and the Apollo Lunar Modules. Uncle Sammy shared how he saved NASA several crucial pounds by redesigning a system without affecting the structural integrity of the unit. Uncle Sammy's name can be found on the moon—along with several astronauts and engineers. He is quite an extraordinary man.

"Houston, we have a problem." Those fateful words were spoken on April 13, 1970. If you watched the actual events unfold on a live televised broadcast, or by viewing the 1995 film Apollo 13, you can grasp the dire circumstances those three astronauts were facing some 200,000 miles from earth.

Massive internal damage to the spacecraft, resulting in a series of unimaginable obstacles, held the lives of those courageous astronauts in the balance. I am beyond proud of my uncle, along with the many other diligent engineers and members of NASA who were instrumental in turning the Apollo Lunar Module into a "lifeboat" and saving the lives of James Lovell, Fred Haise, and Jack Swigert—the crew of Apollo 13.

We all have a story—those moments of joyous elation coupled with our darkest despair, sprinkled with cheerfulness, victories, and lament. These emotions—along with a myriad of personal experiences—form our narrated journey during this life. Filomena Salamone Aquila has a story, one in which a small telling will be chronicled here in this book. She came to this country as a teenager. Her life in Italy was arduous, and her life in America hopeful. Aunt Phyllis is a humble soul, not making much of her unique gifts, accomplishments, or struggles. I see her as courageous and braver than she thinks. On top of all of that, she gives the best hugs—filled with warmth, sunshine, and her whole heart.

The sum of their accomplishments, are not what make Uncle Sammy and Aunt Phyllis so special to me. It is their generosity of spirit, giving hearts, and the love they have freely bestowed upon me and my family that makes me love them so dearly.

When I was a child, Uncle Sammy would captivate me with picturesque portrayals of his life growing up in Brooklyn. When I later had children, he would again unpack these stories for yet another generation. Now that my children are having children, I did not want to lose these precious gifts he would offer through his fashion of oral tradition.

Over the years, I have watched my precious family slip away—and their stories with them. It has been a yearning desire of mine to capture these charming pieces of history in written form, so the generations to come will be able to enjoy a remnant of what I was able to glean firsthand.

The catalyst for this book actually comes to you through my daughter-in-love, Jessica. After a recent family gathering, Jessica remarked to me, that I should have Uncle Sammy write his stories down through an internet site that chronicles a person's life story. I presented this idea to Uncle Sammy—and with a bit of prodding, a little persistence and some encouragement, he agreed to write them down. However, in Uncle Sammy fashion, he did it in a slightly different way and, of course, with excellence. Not only is this book a gift for Uncle Sammy and Aunt Phyllis, but it is also a priceless treasure from them to us—their family and friends.

I love you both dearly;
your adoring niece, Roseann.

"Do you know," Peter asked,
"why swallows build in the eaves of houses?
It is to listen to the stories."

- J. M. Barrie

Contents

SA___ L AQUILA

Part One

The Early Years

Growing Up in Brooklyn, New York

"Delight yourself also in the Lord,
And He shall give you the desires of your heart. "
Psalms 37:4

1

First Day of School

"Education is the period during which you are being instructed
by somebody you do not know,
about something you do not want to know."

— G.K. Chesterton

I was brought up in a household that spoke Italian, because both my parents came from a small town in Calabria called Rosa. They tried to learn English the best they could—and both spoke some broken English. I was raised in this bilingual environment and, in turn, grew up speaking half Italian and half English, as well.

I was about five years old when my parents said, "You are going to school tomorrow." My parents woke me the next day at 7 a.m. to attend first grade at the elementary school located in the Ridgewood section of Brooklyn. Mom and Dad brought me to the school— Halsey Elementary, located on Wilson Avenue—and I entered the class. The teacher asked me a question, and I answered, "Wats a matta fa you?" She then asked me, "What did you say?" So, I repeated, "Wats a matta fa you?" The teacher looked at me and said, "You mean, 'What's the matter with you?'"

What a long day that was for me, it seemed like forever before my mom and dad returned to the school and took me home. The next day, my parents woke me up at 7 a.m. and told me to get ready for school. My answer was, "Not again." What a shocker!

2

La Pistola

"Laughter does good like a medicine."
— Proverbs 17:22

This story happened when I was about six years of age. I came down with the mumps, and the doctor ordered my folks to keep me in bed—otherwise, I could have had complications later on in life. While I was stuck in bed, my sister Phyllis took pity on me and purchased a la pistola for me to play with during my recovery. It was an aluminum target gun with a bullseye target board. The hand gun had an eight-inch-long barrel, a spring-loaded system to accommodate the dart, and a wooden stick with a rubber suction cup at the end. When the dart was loaded into the spring pistol barrel, it was ready to be fired at the target—which was placed at the end of my bed. However, as I started to play with my newfound pardon from boredom, I saw that the dart bounced off the target. So, I decided to put a little bit of saliva on the rubber cup to help it stick to the target.

We lived in an apartment on the third floor that consisted of railroad-type rooms. My father was getting ready for church, he was part of the band and needed to be there by 7 p.m. I was practicing with the pistola, which was loaded, when my father came over to kiss me before leaving the house. As he bent over to kiss me, he accidentally put pressure on the trigger. The pistola went off and made such a noise—whack! —the dart hit my father right in the middle of his forehead. The impact was so strong that my father staggered backward. The dart was still stuck to his head when he stood up straight again. As my father was trying to pull the dart off his forehead—the more he pulled, the more stubborn it stuck—he started to run through the railroad rooms yelling, "Aiutatemi, aiutatemi vi prego," which means, "Please help me" in Italian.

After about 10 minutes of attempting to remove it, the stick at the end of the dart came off. However, the rubber dart remained securely attached to my father's forehead. My mother and sister Phyllis were laughing so hard they literally fell to the floor. After a few minutes of uncontrolled laughter, my mother got up and found a knife from the drawer. She started to pry the rubber suction cup off of my father's forehead. All of a sudden, there was a loud noise and the rubber piece came off. Unfortunately, a small size egg started to grow on my father's forehead. At this point, he was late for church. So, he reached for his fedora—which now rested on the bump—and left for church. WOW!

Type the link below to see and hear Uncle Sammy regale you with this hilarious tale.

https://youtu.be/htYl7MYkAUg

3

The First Call

"Follow me, and I will make you fishers of men."
– Mark 1:17

I n the house on Hancock Street, when I was six years old, I heard from the Lord for the first time—Although, at the time, I didn't know it was Him. One evening, as it was getting late, my father sent me to bed. I was fast asleep when I audibly heard a voice say, "Samuel." The sound was the most beautiful song I had ever heard and the voice filled the entire room like music. The resounding use of my name Samuel, was unfamiliar to my ears as everyone around me called me Sammy. I arose from my bed, went into the kitchen, and asked my parents, "Did you call me?" My father said, "You're dreaming. Go back to sleep." I turned around, went to my room, and fell back asleep. Once again, I was awakened by the same voice calling my name. I got up, ran into the kitchen, and said, "You called me?" My parents replied, "No, you must be dreaming." Again, I went back to bed. For the third time I heard the voice call, Samuel, when I went to the kitchen, I had the same response from my parents. Finally, I went back to bed, and I did not hear His voice again until later in life. At the time, I did not recognize that it was God who was calling me, and I certainly did not know how to answer Him.

My folks converted from Catholicism before I was born, and they were beginning to understand their new journey of faith within the

Pentecostal Church. My parents didn't speak very good English, and they were always with Italian people. Even the church they went to was a Pentecostal-Italian church. The Church of the Savior was where my family attended, which had two locations: The main church, led by Pastor Diglio, was close to Rockaway Blvd, near Atlantic Avenue; and the annex church was a storefront with a large room that had been converted to accommodate church services. The annex was located near our apartment on Hancock Street and Central Avenue. The pastor of the annex church was Pastor Frank Disclafani, who would later become a member of our extended family when my older brother, Johnny, married Pastor Disclafani's daughter, Rosaria—although everyone called her Sadie.

4

Pot Belly Stove

"We would do well to follow our old-fashioned forbears who knew what it was to kneel in breathless, wondering adoration in the presence of God."

– A. W. Tozer

On a very cold evening, during one of the church services, my mother started to dance in the Spirit—which was not at all unusual for her. Mother wore glasses, but when her glasses came off, she couldn't see anything. I remember sitting in the back of the store, where they had a pot belly wood burning stove. You could feel the heat coming off that stove from the back of the store to the front, which was about 35 feet. We had a congregation of about 20 people who would meet there every Wednesday and Friday night. During this meeting, my mother was present, my father played the guitar and sang Gospel songs, and I sat in the back of the church. I was about 7 or 8 years old at the time.

When the Holy Spirit would rest upon my mother, she would start dancing in the Spirit, up and down the aisle. She would go inside the aisle and choose someone to bring to the front. With no glasses, eyes closed, she would dance in the Spirit. This particular evening, while dancing, she came so close to the pot belly stove that her arm laid right on top. It was there for about 2 or 3 minutes, but when she took her arm off that pot belly stove, there was no burn mark and not a single hair on her arm was singed. She just continued dancing in the Spirit. I will never forget that night—it was a miracle. Glory to God!

5

Hot Ovaltine Drink

"Peace begins with a smile."
– Mother Teresa

About year seven, I could go to and from school on my own, and I would routinely come home for lunch in between the school day. My mother was trying to build me up—literally—because I was a skinny little kid. Her method was to sneak two raw eggs into my Ovaltine drink.

I would sit at the kitchen table with my lunch and my Ovaltine drink. When my mother left the kitchen, I would look in the garbage bag—If there were egg shells in the bag, I knew my Ovaltine drink had been fixed with eggs. I would then dump the drink, without my mother's knowledge, and we both left the kitchen with a smile on our faces.

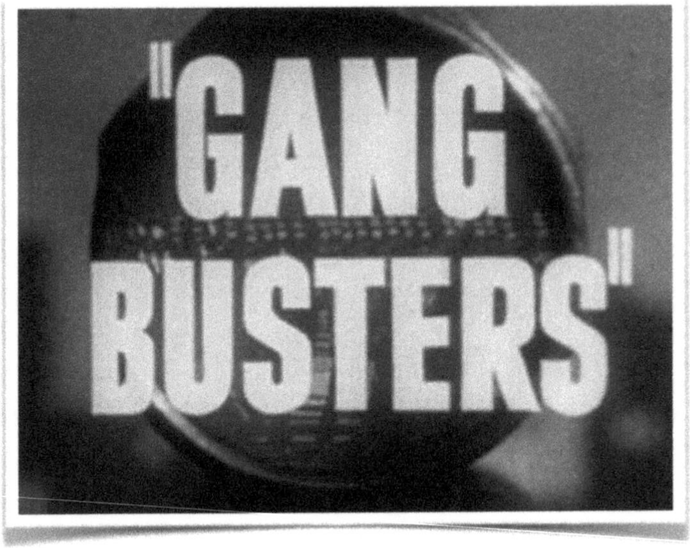
"GANG
BUSTERS"

6

Gang Busters

"Obedience is the highest practical courage."

– Charles Spurgeon

D uring the school week, I liked to watch TV—specifically, a show called *Gang Busters* that ran from 8 p.m. to 9 p.m. My folks did not like this, because they wanted me in bed by 8 p.m. to ensure I got my needed rest. But I was stubborn and would not go to bed. One night, I got them so angry that they ran after me into the dining room. We had a large table, and I went under it. My father got a broom and tried to get me to come out—but I escaped. To add more coal to the fire, so to speak, I shouted at the top of my lungs, "Come and get me coppers!" In the end, though, they did win.

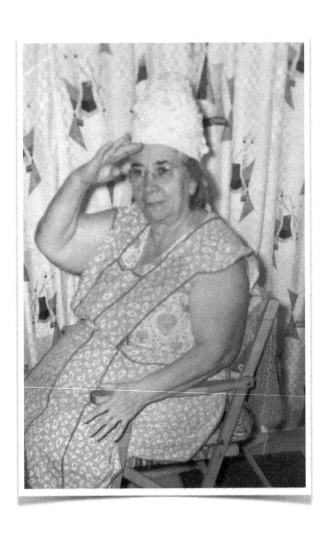

7

Mom the Terminator

"If Mama ain't happy, ain't nobody happy."

My sister Phyllis, my brother John, and myself all had nicknames. Phyllis was "quattro ossa" (4 bones) because she was so skinny, she could hide behind a broom stick. John was "materasso" (mattress) because he was a big boy, and my nickname was "Japanese" because I had buck teeth.

One day, the three of us got our mother so aggravated—I see a trend here—because we were fighting amongst ourselves. She started to run after us through the railroad rooms. We made it to the last room and locked the door, but we could hear our mother breathing very heavily on the other side—knowing she could not wait to get her hands on us.

Our mother was short—low center of gravity—and on the plump side. For the next 10 minutes, John, Phyllis and I noticed it became very quiet on the other side of the door; but we did not unlock the door. All of a sudden, we heard a bang, and then another bang. Our mother had gotten a screwdriver and a hammer and began to take the door off the hinges. Finally, she got the door off and threw it across the room. When she entered the room, I was so scared that I pushed my brother John into her and ran for the hills. In my mind, I concluded my brother could take more of beating than I could.

Noteworthy
My mother was the Terminator,
the enforcer, the disciplinarian.
My dad was like Clark Kent, the well-mannered reporter.

Type the link below to see and hear
Uncle Sammy recite to you
this hilarious tale.

https://youtu.be/ittc4YBb-W4

8

The Frightened Cat

"Fast is fine, but accuracy is everything."

– Wyatt Earp

Supper was being prepared by my mother for the family, and the ingredients were spread out on the kitchen table. As she was preparing and cleaning a salad at the sink, my mother had her back turned away from the table. However, she had a mirror in front of her, which gave her a full view of the kitchen table. Out of nowhere, the pet cat jumped up on the kitchen table, and my mother spotted him through the mirror. In one motion, my mother threw the knife she was using over her shoulder and hit the cat. The cat jumped up about three feet high in the air and ran off. We didn't see the cat for about two weeks. When the cat finally surfaced, he had a slice across his nose—What a shot!

9

Rabbits as Pets

"Hello, Rabbit," he said, "Is that you?"
"Let's pretend it isn't," said Rabbit, "and see what happens."
— A.A. Milne

We lived on the third floor of a building that had a fire escape outside the side window. On this fire escape, we had baby rabbits that we kept in a cage. Every day, my sister Phyllis, my brother John, and myself would feed these pets—and they grew to be large.

One day, my father made supper, and we all sat around the table to eat. Our father asked, "How do you like this chicken?" We said, "OK." He then handed each of us a rabbit's foot for good luck. We looked at each other and ran to the window—there were no rabbits. We started to cry, ran into our bedrooms, locked our doors, and cried all night.

Part Two

The Teenage Days

Growing Up in Brooklyn, New York

"Sometimes you will never know the value of a moment until it becomes a memory."

– Dr. Seuss

10

Adventures with Nelma

"If everything seems under control, you're not going fast enough."
– Mario Andretti

I was in desperate need of a haircut—my hair was so long, it was hanging over my ears. My brother John was about to take me to the barber, when my older sister Nelma, who was at the house visiting, said, "Oh, I can give you a haircut! I do a lot of haircuts. You don't have to worry about it."

So, I sat on a chair, while Nelma came over with the scissors and a comb. She then put a towel around my neck, and I thought— "Oh, she must know what she is doing." In the middle of the haircut, Nelma reached for a salad bowl, and put it on my head. It was all over in about twenty minutes. As she removed the salad bowl from my head, I heard a loud gasp and some moans and groans coming from my mother and John. My brother immediately put a baseball cap on my head and took me to the barber. When we arrived, I removed my cap, and the barber looked at me and said, "Who scalped you?" He then proceeded to shave my entire head—It was so bad!

Nelma had many talents, beside cutting hair, she was a world-class baker. She would often make me my favorite dessert, banana cream pie, and bring it over to mom and pops house. She could also have driven for NASCAR!

One day, when Nelma was coming up the stairs to see the family, I was going down from the apartment. When we meet on the stairs, she asked me where I was going—I told her I was heading to Broadway, which was only two blocks away. Nelma replied, "I'll drop you off." I got in the car and had barely shut the door before I had to open it again, because we were there already. The tires never did touch the ground. Nelma had a heavy foot—if you were behind the car when she started the engine, she'd suck you up the tailpipe.

Noteworthy
The moral of the story:
Go to the barber for a great haircut.

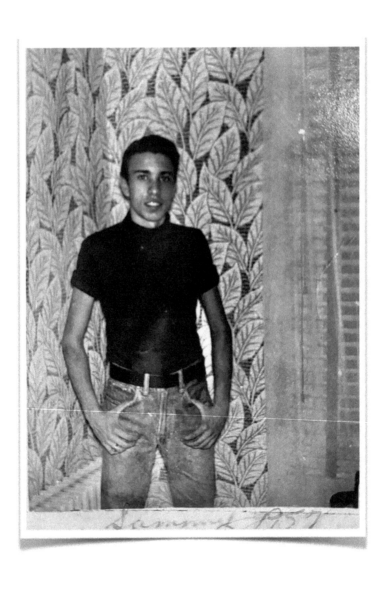

Sammy 1957

11

Curly Hair

"Oh, the cleverness of me!"

– J. M. Barrie

This anecdote takes place when I was around the age of twelve and had straight, brown hair. When I was in school, I noticed a few of my classmates had wavy-curly hair, and I wished I had wavy-curly hair.

Around this same time, my sister Nelma's children, Carmelita and Carol, were staying with us at our house. Both my nieces knew I wanted curly hair, so they said, "We will set your hair with bobby pins overnight and then remove them before you go to school, and then you will have curly hair." They proceeded to put bobby pins all throughout my hair, which took about an hour. That was a restless night. I could not sleep because I was being pinched all evening by those pins. The next morning when I got up, Carmelita and Carol removed all the bobby pins from my hair and—oh boy—did I have CURLY hair. It was so bad that I looked like little orphan Annie. No matter what I tried, I could not get those curls out. I did not go to school for three days—What a bummer!

12

Two Strikes You're Out

"If you can't find the key to success, pick the lock."

– Unknown

A motorcycle jacket and a pair of powder blue peg pants with a fancy silver buckle—That's what I wore at age seventeen.

I went out one evening and met my friends at the local candy store, which was a few hundred feet from my house. While at the candy store, we all decided to walk up to Broadway, about ten of us in all. We went to where the Broadway L was by the overhead transient system.

The pack of us were all standing in front of the candy store talking when suddenly a patrol car, the local 53, pulled up and stopped in front of the store. The police officer pointed into the crowd, where the ten of us were all gathered around, and he gestured with his finger—like a hook— and said, "Come here, come here, come here." Everybody parted, which left me standing in the middle by myself, as the officer said, "Yes, you." I walked all the way over to the street where he parked his patrol car and noticed two officers in the vehicle. One of the officers told me to get in the back of the car, so I did.

He said, "What are you doing over here?"

I responded, "Well, I'm just hanging out with my friends." He said to me, "You got any ID?" So, I said, "Ya." I showed him whatever I had as an ID, and the officer said, "Well, you look like somebody that's from a gang. A leader that we have been looking for." "Oh ya?" I said—I'm thinking in my head, "That's beautiful." "Well," he continued, "You oughta just go home." So, I got out of the back of the patrol car and headed to where my ten friends were standing on the street.

At this point, we all went back to Hancock Street and Evergreen Avenue. On that corner, there was a candy store, a garment factory, and a sewing machine place. We all gathered in a circle again. I was up against the door to the garment factory, which was closed because it was after hours, when I noticed the lock on the door looked very familiar. I said to my friend, "That lock looks just like the lock on my bicycle. I made a skeleton key to open up my bicycle lock, I wondered if this key fits in this lock as well." As I stuck the key into the lock and discovered it sure enough fit, the same cop car with the same two police officers came around the corner of Hancock and Evergreen Avenue.

As if on cue, everybody parts and I was standing in the middle with the key in my hand. The police officer pointed to me again, gesturing with his finger—like a hook—to come back over to where he was. I walked over to where the officers were parked and, just like before, they told me to get into the back of the patrol car. So, I climbed into the back of the police car again.

The officer looked at me, and for the second time that night, asked me what I was doing. So, I explained, "I was just curious that the lock on the door is the same lock I have on my bicycle. I made a skeleton key for my bicycle, and I was eager to see if my key fit that lock." He looked at me and said, "Son, you better go home. You got two strikes against you right now." So, I got out of the car, and this time—I went home.

Part Three

The Working Years

Growing Up in Brooklyn, New York

"I have always felt life first as a story; and if there is a story there is a storyteller."

– G.K. Chesterton

Frank, Phyllis, Theresa, Lynn, Camela, Sam, Ralph, & Sadie

13

Famiglia

"Send them my love—
that's L-O-V-E, with a hug at the end."
– Sam Aquila

My father, Ralph Aquila, owned his own shoe repair business in Connecticut, before we moved to New York. In those days, it was cheaper to repair a shoe than buy a new pair. When we moved to New York, my father took a job with a shoe company as a leveler—the one who puts the curve in your sole. He would work on this machine that you could see from a mile away, inside the factory. Dad would be going up and down on this machine, shaping and leveling the shoes.

In fact, almost everybody in the family worked at the shoe factory for a while—including my brother Lynn, Phyllis, John, and myself. We all worked different jobs. I was a tack puller on soles. Lynn would cement the soles together and get them ready for the stitcher. I can't remember Phyllis and John's jobs, but we all put in our time at the shoe factory.

In those days, large families stuck together. Many families worked in a local area, within 10 miles of their homes. I wanted the best for my family and tried to help wherever I could. I remember trying to help my brothers, Veto and John, by getting them a job in the engineering field with me. I endeavored to oversee both my brothers as drafters, but their minds didn't seem to be on drafting—It was a complicated business. Nonetheless, I tried to teach them how to work this new trade. My brothers would be working under me, I could supervise their work, give them small tasks to do, and offer a better salary than they were making. But engineering was not for them, however, that's what brothers do for each other—that's what family does. They help one another, they give one-another a leg up, they are there to support each other, through the good times and the bad.

My brother Johnny and I were close—Not only was he the best-man at my wedding, he also offered his band and his musical skills with his Gretsch guitar, as a gift to Phyllis and I for our reception. We were buddies, partners in pranks, and we both enjoyed the art of instigating. I remember this one time when John was—once again—picking on our sister, Phyllis. They were playing in the street when she got so mad at him, she attempted to push him down the street sewer. Johnny was a big guy and would never fit down the sewer—but Phyllis tried anyway. You could hear her yelling from down the block, "Get down there with all the other rats!"

One afternoon, John and I were sitting in the living room on the couch, while our mother was crocheting. My mother was always crocheting something, and Johnny was in the habit of teasing her when she crocheted. He was fooling around with the crochet needle, and I didn't know he had the needle next to him when I threw a pillow at him. The pillow hit his hand, and the crochet needle got stuck in his chest—Yikes! My mother had to get the needle out of his chest. It didn't go deep—but it did draw blood.

John signed up for the Navy—which was odd to me, because he didn't like to swim or go in the water, but he joined the Navy anyway. I will never forget the time God watched over him in the

Navy. He was transferred from the minesweeper he was on and reassigned to an Auk-class minesweeper. John never asked for the transfer, but they transferred him anyway. A short time later, the mine sweeper he was formally stationed on, hit an ocean mine. There was quite a bit of damage to the ship, and many lives were lost. I thanked God for His hand of protection over my brother. The pacific seas were ladened with thousands of these mines from a decade of warfare. Johnny, along with the Navel crew of the Auk-class minesweeper, were tasked with the enormous and dangerous work, of clearing the seas, we sail so freely today.

Johnny entertaining the family around the table

When John came home from the Navy, he wanted to make me a knish from scratch. He knew I liked knishes, because I used to frequent this Greek place on Broadway that sold knishes and frankfurters. Johnny was laboring in the kitchen for a while making those knishes. When he finally placed them on the table, they were like hockey pucks. You couldn't bite into them—and if you did, you left your teeth there in the knish.

Every Sunday, all the family got together at my mother and father's house. My mom would make pasta and meatballs, and we would sit around the table—eating, laughing, telling stories and spinning yarns. All the family was there, even our cats and dogs.

You know, when the Italian people sit at the table, it's about four hours—which of course includes a never-ending feast.

My father was not only skilled in making shoes, but in playing different musical instruments as well. He passed on his gift of musical artistry to John, when he taught him how to play the guitar. After John and Sadie were married, my dad taught Sadie how to play the mandolin. We used our gifts and talents in church. I remember being about six years old, singing in Italiano on stage, while John would strum the guitar and my father would play the mandolin, during church services.

Noteworthy
My brothers Veto, Lynn & John
all signed up and served
in the United States Armed Services

John Aquila
U.S. Navy, WWII

"The true soldier fights not because he hates what is in front of him, but because he loves what is behind him."

– G.K. Chesterton

14

Canary Yellow

"Many are the plans in a man's heart,
but it is the Lord's purpose that prevails."

– Proverbs 19:21

At the age of 21, I started thinking about buying a brand new 1957 Ford Fairlane 500. However, I was at the age when a young man could be drafted into the service. So, I thought to myself, "Before I buy this car, I am going to go up to the draft board to see if they can tell me my chances of being drafted, before I invest money into a new car."

So, I went up to the draft board, which was located on the other side of Broadway and Hancock Street. When I entered the building, I asked the clerk to find out when—or even if—I would be called up for duty. He looked my name up and replied, "Nah, don't worry about it, they're probably not even going to call you; you're too far down the stream." I said, "Good, that's great news."

I left the draft board, went home, and said to myself, "Ok, I think I am going to buy this car." My brother Veto was working as a foreman at the Ford place on Bushwick Avenue, so I went down to the Ford place and bought the car. Canary yellow and black—it was a beautiful car. Everybody noticed it when I drove by. It was indeed a good-looking car—and all the girls knew it.

There I was, with my new car, which I had for about a month or so, when I received an order to report for induction. A letter from the draft board announcing they were drafting me; they pushed my card up—I just bought this brand-new car and I was now being drafted by the U.S. Army. I had just missed the Korean conflict by the time they called me in, so I'm not sure why I was even drafted so suddenly. I went for my physical, at the designated time and place that was stated in the letter, and—just like that, I was in the Army now! I was assigned to Fort Dix for a bit, and then I was transferred to Virginia, where attended engineering school.

Every once in a while, they would give you a 75-mile pass, where you could travel up to 75 miles away. When I got the pass, I decided to go all the way home on the bus from Virginia. When I got home, I decided to take my canary yellow and black 1957 Ford Fairlane back to the base in Virginia, where I was stationed. When I finally arrived at the base, it was early morning, and they were already calling reveille. I was in my civilian clothes, and I had to park the car and run all the way to the barracks to change my clothes. When I finally made it, I was the last one to get in line for reveille.

On this particular day at Fort Dix, when they called reveille, a big, heavy-set sergeant came along and said, "Hey you, killa, killa." He was pointing to me, and I said, "You mean, 'Aquila?'" He replied, "Ya! You, killa, come here. You got KP duty, and you're gonna be in the KP kitchen today."

I walked into the kitchen at Fort Dix, which was a consolidated mess hall—they fed 10,000 soldiers there. The kitchen was so big that they had tables, three levels high, filled with dead chickens. There must have been thousands of chickens there. They gave me a hatchet and a knife, that you couldn't even kill yourself with it was so dull. I had to clean the chickens, take out the guts, and put them in a plastic bag. There were so many chickens stacked, they were falling off the tables onto the ground and I was kicking them with my foot. I did that all day long, from about 8 a.m. to 4 a.m. the next day.

I smelled like a chicken for weeks after that. I scrubbed myself down in the shower, and I still could not get that smell off of me for weeks and weeks. I had no desire to eat chicken after that. As soon as I saw chicken, that poignant smell returned in my nostrils—and that was all I needed to refuse the fowl.

There is a terrible odor, that permeates your nostrils, when you are taking the guts out of a chicken and trying to put the livers and innards in a plastic bag. I can still smell the stench of those chickens even now, as I retell this story.

We then had to cut up the chickens, as well as take the legs off and chop them in half. However, the tools they gave us were useless. I couldn't chop anything with those knives. You couldn't commit Harakiri with them, they were so dull.

They also had huge pots—about 3 feet high and 2 feet in diameter—to stir the contents in these enormous pots, they gave you something like a canoe oar. Some people got to peel potatoes—but I had to cut up the chickens all day.

Noteworthy
Sam can speak:
English, Deutsche, Français and un po 'di Italiano
also…
Chicken is <u>*Not*</u> his dish!

While in France, I met my childhood buddy, Carmine.
He was stationed in the same outfit as myself, in Verdon, France.
We had gone to Sunday school together as kids, back in Brooklyn.

15

Susi Mi Signore

*"Open my heart and you will see
Graved inside of it, 'Italy.'"*

– Robert Browning

A fter a period of time at Fort Belvoir, I was slotted to return home due to my parent's ailing health. I had asked Pastor Diglio, of my church back home—to write a letter to the Army, asking them to station me closer to our home in Brooklyn. I heard back from the army, saying, they would get me situated not far from our house, most likely Fort Dix, New Jersey. I remember waiving arrivederci to the Statue Liberty, as I was going out on a troop carrier headed to Europe and thinking, "I am never going to make it back."

When I arrived in Europe, the Army stationed me at Bremerhaven, Germany. From Germany, I was moved to France—where I fulfilled the rest of my service. While in France, I had a chance to visit other countries, such as Italy. I had some good times and, although I would have rather been at home, you just make the best of the situation you are in.

The Army had given me a pass for a 15-day leave. I had two friends with me, and we had a civilian car. We were stationed in

France at the time, so we said, "Let's go to Italy." One of the guys I was traveling with, had friends and relatives in Italy, and I had relatives in Italy, as well. We got on the parkway and drove through the Swiss Mountains, which took four hours to go up and four hours to come down.

I said to these guys, "The first town we are probably going to hit is Torino, and most likely, everyone there will have black hair." Imagine my surprise when we got to the bottom of the mountain into Torino and everyone had blonde hair, nobody had black hair. From there, we traveled to the center of Rome, where there were seven roads going out and no signs. We were all at a loss, and I didn't know which way to go. I told my buddies I didn't know where the street to Calabria was, nor did my friend who also had relatives there.

The one thing I knew for sure—we needed directions. I got out of the US Chevy car we were driving, and looked around the streets for someone to help us. Way off in the distance, what seemed like a mile away, I noticed this guy wearing a black fedora hat and a cape around his shoulders, sitting on a bench. It took me about 10 minutes to finally reach him. As I stood in front of him, I said—in my best Italian, "Susi a de mi signore, ma dov'e` la strada per la Cosenza." Then, in perfect English, he said, "Well, where do you want to go, sonny?" He pointed me to the right road, and off we went to Cosenza, where I met my uncle on my mother's side. We stayed down there about 15 days. When we traveled back to Orléans, France, we were broke. We had given away all of our money, we were moved with such compassion for our family, who they didn't have much. When we returned, we maybe had $5 dollars between the three of us.

When I entered the Army, I was an E1, by the end of the first two years, I was as an E3, Specialist Third Class. I served in the US Army for two years active duty and four years inactive duty. After the last four years, I was promoted to a Sergeant, E4.

Noteworthy
Orléans, France ~ Torino, Italy 481mi - 7hr 18min
Torino ~ Rome 433mi - 7hr
Rome ~ Cosenza 324 mi - 4hr 52 min
Orléans, France ~ Calabria, Italy 1276 mi - 19 hr 7m

16

Se Non Lavori Non Mangi

"Scientists study the world as it is;
Engineers create the world that never has been."
– Theodore von Karman

W hen I was 19, I left the shoemaking business and went on to get my first job as a draftsman with Tagg Design. I was there about six months to a year, when I was hired on at the Atlantic Design Company as a design draftsman. At that time, companies were giving you terrific salaries to come work for them. So, I left the Atlantic Design Company and got a job at another design company, Devanco Inc. They paid me quite a bit more than the previous drafting companies. While I was working for Devanco, I got drafted into the Army—and they did not pay nearly as well.

When I was home from the service—about three days—I decided to visit some friends, who worked for the Atlantic Design Company. When I worked for them, they were located in New York; however, they had moved to New Jersey. So, I took a trip to New Jersey to say hello to some old friends at the design company. While I was there, my old manager came out to speak to me. He then went over to the personnel manager, who came out to see me and said, "How would you like to work for us?" I accepted the job, they hired me that day, and they told me they wanted me to start on Monday.

When I moved to Bellmore, New York, it was further out on the island. As I mentioned before, the Atlantic Design Company had moved to New Jersey, which meant I had to travel two hours to work and two hours home. My routine was to get up at 5 a.m.; take my car from Bellmore and drive to the Eastern Parkway, where the trains were; park my car underneath the elevator; go up and walk across; take the 8th Avenue Line into New York City to Chamber Street. Then, I would walk from Chamber Street to the Hudson tubes, where I would take the tubes to Newark, NJ. If I had enough time to wait for the bus, I would take the bus to Broad Street. If I missed that connection, I would walk it. Finally—after about 2 years of doing this 4-hour commute—they opened up the office in New York again, and I was able to go back to that office—which cut my time travel to an hour and twenty minutes.

I remember trying to make subway connections at 5 o'clock. People would come running down from Chamber Street to get to the subway station. You could feel the whole station shake. You needed to stand next to a steel beam to hold onto it, or you would be knocked over onto the tracks. The people were like cattle running down those stairs, trying to make their connections.

"Opportunity is missed by most people
because it is dressed in overalls and looks like work."
– Thomas Edison

Phyllis & Sam Aquila
May 13, 1961

17

How I Met My Wife, Filomena

"We proclaim the prophetic grace of marriage when we understand the sacredness of building a history together."
— Gary Thomas, Sacred Marriage

O ctober 1959, I was honorably discharged from the Army at the age of twenty-four.

Home several weeks from the Army, I decided to attend church services at the Church of the Savior. The main building, led by Pastor Diglio, was located on Gunter Place, on Rockaway Avenue near Atlantic Blvd in Brooklyn. The second church was a store front location, on Hancock St. and Central Ave—this was the Annex Church, which was led by Pastor Frank Disclafani.

The main church had two Sunday services—one in English at 11 a.m. and another in Italian on Sunday evening. I attended the 11 a.m. service in English. On this particular Sunday, Pastor Diglio, inquired of the congregation who wanted to be baptized in water on the upcoming Saturday. I raised my hand, along with nine other people. The pastor asked the same question during the Sunday evening Italian service and ten people raised their hands, including Filomena.

Saturday came around and the water baptism service was to begin downstairs on the first floor, where the water tank was located. The congregation filled up the church, and the people to be baptized were to begin showing up. Nineteen people—between the two services, raised their hands be baptized, however, only myself and Filomena showed up. She was on one side of the room, and I was on the other.

Neither Filomena nor myself had ever met before, we were strangers to each other. Pastor Disclafani, was the pastor who led the baptismal services for the Church. As he began to officiate the service, he motioned that I would be the first to be baptized. At that point, I proceeded to the changing room and put on a robe and then I entered the baptismal tank. The pastor submerged me into the water, and as he raised me up, he was looking at Filomena—who was waiting to be baptized next—at that moment he said to me, "Here comes your wife."—Revelation.

The next day, as I was sitting in my house, when who walks in the door—Filomena and her neighbor, who had stopped by the house to visit my mother. I was interested in Filomena, so I asked her on a date. We communicated quite well, she spoke to me in Italian, and I answered her in English. Within a month, my heart was captivated by her, I knew I wanted to marry Filomena. I asked her to marry me, she said yes, and 11 months later we were married on May 13, 1961.

"You have captured my heart, my treasure, my bride.
You hold it hostage with one glance of your eyes."

– Song of Songs 4:9

Carmela, Ralphie & Ralph

18

Past to Present... A Lasting Legacy

"Every time we make the decision to love someone, we open
ourselves to great suffering, because those we love cause us
not just great joy but also great pain. The greatest pain
comes from leaving. When the child leaves home; when
the husband or wife leaves for a long period of time
or for good, when the beloved friend departs to another
country or dies...the pain of the leaving can tear us apart.
Still, if we want to avoid the suffering of leaving, we will never
experience the joy of loving. And love is stronger than fear,
life stronger than death, hope stronger than despair. We have
to trust that the risk of loving is always worth taking."

– Henri Nouwen

Once upon a time, there lived a remarkable generation—

An age of people who did not throw things away, instead, they fixed them and made the broken pieces work again. The same was true for their marriages and relationships. They had a strong sense of commitment, loyalty, and family; and they honored

God with reverence. These courageous individuals did not choose the hard road, but they certainly were not afraid to travel it.

While compiling this book, Uncle Sammy, once again, captivated me with picturesque recitals of stories I had not been privy to before starting this project. One particular story was that of my grandmother, Carmela Aquila—or "the terminator," as Uncle Sammy so affectionately called her in Chapter 5.

Grandma Aquila had a strength that survived hardship and sorrow—some of which wounded so deeply a soul, it would have caused many to lose all hope. But alas, she did not. She came to America from Italy, where she could speak no English and somehow managed to live with little way to communicate with the new world around her. She gave birth to fifteen children, of which only seven survived to adulthood—some died at birth, while others lived to be a little older and then were gone. How do you rise up each day after that type of unspeakable sorrow? Is there ever a time, when mourning ceases and life begins again? This strength of fortitude Grandma Aquila had, was not self-produced but, as you have read, was developed and poured out, over a lifetime of intimate moments with God, His strength and His grace.

Equally astonishing were the stories of how grandma praised and worshiped God—how she danced before the Lord, as David did, in 2 Samuel, chapter 6. I began a quest to uncover some enlightenment into their unique perspective on moving forward and living after such great loss. While studying, I came across some thought-provoking information. Suffering was very much a part of the human experience before the 1900's. There were two factors that altered this reality—the development of anesthetic around the 1830's, and the development of aspirin during the 1890's. What does this mean and how does this relate? I am so glad you inquired. I shall lend that explanation to Os Guinness, English author and social critic:

"Modernity has minimized pain, and of course that is good. Around 1900 historians tell us, for the first time in human history, an adult could live most of their lives without any significant pain and that's wonderful, but there is a downside that is behind the pollyannaism of many modern people. They have not suffered; they have not seen death." – Os Guinness, Ph.D.

Corrie ten Boom, Mother Teresa, Dietrich Bonhoeffer, Joni Eareckson Tada, and countless others had me realizing, like my grandparents, these people were not consumers of God—they were servants of God. Franny Crosby, who was not a stranger to heartbreak or traumatic life struggles, did not allow her blindness to overshadow her many God given abilities. She was dubbed, "The Blind Poetess" and declared, "I want to lift people's souls toward Jesus and Salvation, not to coddle them with false warmth." Dr. Timothy Keller wrote, "A true servant serves God for God; they do not serve God for what they are getting out of it. In times of suffering, we will see whether you got into that relationship with God, to get God to serve you, or whether you got into that relationship in order to serve Him—out of love and gratitude for all He is, and all He has done." This is certainly a difficult and weighty statement, but one my grandparents must have known decades before Tim Keller ever penned it.

One may never know the depth of afflictions my grandparents truly endured—the hardships they fought through and overcame, in order to give their children opportunities that were not available for themselves.

The stories I have discovered through writing this book have made me keenly aware, and even more grateful, for the rich heritage of faithful men and women who forged a trail and paved it with prayer before me. It has, in a sense, connected some dots for me in my own life. My grandparents left a legacy, not of wealth or fame, but of something that could never be lost or taken away. They left the legacy of a strong faith in God and of a life that would live forever in eternity. I am beholden to my Uncle Sammy for sharing such priceless and intimate memories with me.

"Marriage requires a radical commitment to love our spouses as they are, while longing for them to be what they are not yet. Every marriage moves either toward enhancing one another's glory or toward degrading each other."

– Dan Allender, Ph.D

Carmela, Filomena, & Ralph

Filomena with her dad & stepmom

Thy beauty filleth the very air, Never saw I a woman so fair."
– George MacDonald

"For God created the marriage relationship to point to a greater reality. From the moment marriage was instituted, God aimed to give the world an illustration of the Gospel."
– Juli Slattery, Rethinking Sexuality

John & Sadie's 25th Anniversary, Phyllis & Frank

Phyllis, John, Sam and Ralph

*The grandchildren Celebrating Grandpa Aquila
on his 80th Birthday*

Ruth, Ralph & Susan

Phyllis creating an exquisite wedding dress for her daughter

Sammy wowing the crowd with one of his famous card tricks

Type the link below to experience Sam soaring to new heights...

https://youtu.be/SrF-e5H8FnU

Beautifully dancing together as Husband & Wife
May 13, 1961

Beautifully dancing together again, as one of the longest married couples during Christian & Jessica's Wedding
September 30, 2017

May 13, 1961

May 30, 2021

Uncle Sammy & Aunt Phyllis, passing on a rich heritage of love and faithfulness to their great, great nephews, Christian & Oaklen

Taking a break from writing, at a favorite Italian restaurant

"What greater thing is there for two human souls, than to feel that they are joined for life——to strengthen each other in all labor, to rest on each other in all sorrow, to minister to each other in all pain, to be one with each other in silent unspeakable memories at the moment of the last parting?"

– George Eliot

Part Four

The Senior Ministry Years

Growing Up in Brooklyn, New York

*"Our greatest impact in life will be made
not among the masses
but in the few people we pour our life into.*
— Dan Spader

Street Ministry – Walmart Parking Lot

Gospel Singers
E.W. Bass - lead singer
Wendy Bass - key board
Molly Sexton
Don &Connie Hiner
Joe & Miriam Luszik
Pastor Allen Beck (rep Sun City Center Christian Church)
Sam & Phyllis (rep Destiny Church)

19

The Call to Ministry and Personal Healing

"God does not call those who are equipped,
He equips those whom He has called."
— Smith Wigglesworth

I retired from the workforce in 1998, and in 1999 my wife and I moved to Florida. During that time, I was diagnosed with prostate cancer—but God had other plans! Phyllis and I attended a Spirit-filled church in Parrish, called the Light House. When we started attending the Light House, we sat in the last row in the back, right next to the exit. "First one out," I thought. I remember telling Phyllis that I loved the worship songs, and I could listen to them all day.

One Sunday, the church had a guest speaker, Randi Lecher, from The School of the Holy Spirit, who prophesied over the people in the congregation. Randi walked to the back of the church, stood right beside me, and said, "Do you know you are in need of a healing?" I said, "Yes." He asked me to stand up and inquired after my name, to which I replied, "Samuel." Randi repeated my name and said this to me, "God's going to heal you of your infirmity and extend your life, and No-No-No-No, you're not going to sit around and listen to the music. God is going to use you and your wife in ministry."

Two to three months later, the church had another guest speaker, Ron Campbell, a prophet of God. Once again, my wife and I sat in that same back row, right by the exit. Ron pointed to the back of the church and said, "The couple sitting in the back," and I turned around to find there was no one behind us. He said, "Yes. You." He then began to prophesy over Phyllis and myself. He declared, "God will use you in ministry as an Evangelist, and whoever you pray for and lift up to God, He will honor it." While I was attending the Light House Church, I received the Baptism of the Holy Spirit.

Today, 23 years later, I am still operating in the office of Evangelism, and I have continued preaching and teaching the word of God. I am still free of prostate cancer, and my PSA reading is less than one. If God can heal me, He can heal you! God is no respecter of persons, and nothing is impossible with God.

This is my testimony—to God be all the Glory!

Sam, Pat Molly - Prison Chaplin, The Garrett's

20

Miracles, Signs, and Wonders

"You are not learning the Word,
You are [coming] to encounter the Word"

– Ken Brown

The year was 2003, I was invited to speak at a special gathering of The Full Gospel Business Men's Meeting, which included their wives. I was setting up the sound equipment, surrounded by the members, when an elderly lady walked in out of the blue. She had a limp and was walking with a cane, because one leg was shorter than the other. She pushed her way through the members and stopped in front of me. Putting her finger on my chest, she proceeded to declare, "I have come for my healing." I was stunned by her statement and actually took a step back.

When an altar call was given, this elderly lady made her way up to the front, by the altar, limping with her cane. When I prayed with her, the anointing of God and His overwhelming presence were so strong, she was not able to stand and fell to the floor (slain in the Spirit), where she lay for the rest of the evening. Toward the end of the service, she arose from the floor and walked away—with no cane and no limp!

To God be all the Glory!

"In brief, the teaching of the New Testament, is that the outpouring at Pentecost was the historic beginning of an era which was to be characterized by a continuous outpouring of the Holy Spirit."
                                        – A.W. Tozer,

21

Book of Acts Experience

"Being filled with the Spirit is simply this–having my whole nature yielded to His power. When the whole soul is yielded to the Holy Spirit, God Himself will fill it."

– Andrew Murray

Phyllis and I were introduced to the prison ministry by E.W. Bass and his daughter-in-law, Wendy Bass in 2003. We felt as though we were specifically called to this ministry, and from the years 2003 through 2012, my wife and I ministered at the Manatee Prison. On the first Sunday of each month, we would go to the Manatee Omega (10) maximum security prison and conduct a church service in the A, B, and C blocks. The second Sunday of each month, we would conduct a church service at the Boot Camp and the Academy.

In preparation for Sunday service, I spent Saturday evening in my bedroom, preparing my message for the Sunday visit to the Academy. I remember this particular Saturday night so vividly. I asked the Lord what He wanted me to say to these men, who had already accepted the Lord and had been baptized by water. In a voice that surrounded me, the Lord said, "Teach them about the Holy Spirit." Tears started to stream down my face and splashed onto my Bible—I couldn't utter a word. Later that evening, I was able to put together the Sunday message entitled, Who is the Holy Spirit?

The next day, we were on our way to the Academy, which was a single level building, opposite the Omega (10) complex. It stood approximately 50 feet wide and 100 feet long. We entered the building with our equipment, and inside the hallway, we set up our sound equipment. The prison cells ran down each side of the hallway the entire length of the building. As the men came out of their cells, the guards made three lines in the hallway, which was about 20 feet wide, and sat them down there in the hallway. We were allotted one hour to conduct our church service, which consisted of worship and my message, "Who is the Holy Spirit." By the time I finished speaking, our time was up and did not allow for me to follow up with these men.

The second time we went to the Academy, I brought a dear friend with me, Pastor Peter Novellino. However, I did not discuss with him the message I delivered the previous month. Pastor Novellino preached a message on the "Gifts of the Holy Spirit." When he finished speaking, our time was up and, once again, I was not able to follow up with the men.

The third time we went, I brought my daughter Ruth, who is an ordained minister, along with some of her friends from her church. Once again, I did not mention to them what I had previously spoken to the men about. Ruth delivered her message to the men, which was also about the Holy Spirit. When she was finished, we had about fifteen minutes left. I stepped forward and asked the men if anyone would like to be baptized in the Holy Spirit. All three rows of men stood up. I thought to myself, "I'll start at the back of the hallway and come forward." As I walked to the back, I felt a wave of electricity come from behind me. All of a sudden, the men started to fall all around me. From the front to the back of the hallway, the men were slain in the Spirit. I could see underneath them as they bounced up and down like basketballs. They were speaking in unknown tongues, and their facial complexions had entirely transformed. I was the only one left standing in the middle of the hallway as the guards proceeded to come out of their security room. Phyllis and Ruth hurried to where I was standing and uttered, "They are going to throw us out." The tall, muscular guards approached me, they had their hands on their weapons. As I looked up at these large and capable guards, one of them put their hand on my shoulder and said, "Sir, you take as much time as you need."

This is my testimony—to God be all the Glory!

You are our letter, known and read by everyone,
written not in ink, but with the Spirit of the living God,
not on stone tablets, but on the tablets of human hearts.
– 2 Corinthians 3:2-3

Manatee County Prison
Boot Camp Academy, Security Guards
Ministry Personnel

Academy preparing for water baptism

Academy Water Baptism
During 2003-2012, under the leadership of E.W. Bass
500 men accepted the Lord as Savior and were baptized in water.

"Therefore go and make disciples of all nations, baptizing them in the name of the Father and of the Son and of the Holy Spirit, and teaching them to obey everything I have commanded you. And surely, I am with you always, to the very end of the age."
– Matthew 28:19-20

Home Bible Study
21st Century Discipleship Training Course
Genesis – Revelations

"Christianity, if false, is of no importance,
and if true, of infinite importance.
The only thing it cannot be is moderately important."
– C.S. Lewis

Plaza west Health Center, Nursing Home

Palm Gardens, Nursing Home

"Baptism is faith in action" – Watchman Nee

"Perhaps the transformation of the disciples of Jesus is the greatest evidence of all for the Resurrection." –John Stott

Abbreviated Biography of Samuel Aquila

Samuel was born in Brooklyn, New York. He was one of fifteen children, of which seven survived:, Veto, Orlando, (or Lynn), Pat, Nelma, Phyllis, John, (or Johnny) and Samuel.
Samuel was educated at a technical high school,
Manhattan Technical Institute, where he studied drafting and machine design;
Fort Belvoir Engineering School for soil engineering;
State University of New York for an ATCF-AAS-degree in Mechanical Technology

His various employment and places of work include:
Tagg Design as a draftsman;
Atlantic Design Co. as a design draftsman;
Denvenco, Inc. as a design draftsman;
U.S. Army as a soil engineer;
New York City; and Bethpage, Long Island;
Consultants & Designers Inc.;
Grumman Aerospace Corp. as a structural design engineer;
Schenck Trebel Corp. of Deer Park as a senior project engineer;
Vice President of Asgard Mechanical Systems;
President of Alpha & Omega Mechanical Systems

His jobs have placed him in: Germany, Mexico, Connecticut, and NASA—where he received the Certificate of Participation Award in the Lunar Module Program of Project APOLLO
On Nov 14, 1999, God called he and his wife into ministry.

Sam and Filomena have three grown children and now live in Sun City Center, where they are involved in the following ministries:

Prison Ministry – Manatee Co. Boot Camp & Academy

Prison Ministry – Manatee Co. Omega 10 Max Security

Prison Ministry – Hillsbourgh Correctional Facility for Women

Palm Gardens - Nursing Home,

Sun Terrace Nursing Home

Plaza West Health Center

Home Bible Study-21st Discipleship Training Course–Genesis thru Revelations

Full Gospel Business Men's Fellowship International, Vice President & Secretary of Treasure, Ruskin Chapter (2004-2005)

"Not that the story need be long, but it will
take a long while to make it short."
                              – Henry David Thoreau

Phyllis in Pietrelcina, Italy

Abbreviated Biography of Filomena Aquila

Filomena was born as Filomena Salamone in a small town in Italy called Pietrelcina—a providence of Benevente, near Naples.
Her mother's name was Assunta, her father's name was Orlando, and she had one brother named Cosmo.
Filomena lived on a farm, and most of the work fell upon her and her brother—a tough life at a young age.
Filomena's parents were unable to help. Her mother was confined to bed with a serious illness, and her father was a prisoner of war during WWII.
Filomena came to Brooklyn, New York in 1958.
She lived in a house located on Atlantic Avenue and Rockaway Boulevard.

Filomena found work in the garment industry, as follows:

1. Coat Factory as a floor lady
2. Dress Factory as a seamstress and dress designer
3. Dress Factory as a pattern maker

Promise me you'll always remember: You're braver than you believe, and stronger than you seem, and smarter than you think.

– A. A. Milne

Thank you, Father God, for allowing us to minister to your people, in the name of Jesus Christ. Father God, we give you all the honor and glory in Jesus name.

Your humble servants, Sam & Phyllis.

We all face the end of this life——
Everyone walks through that door, nobody holds
your hand and goes with you, you walk through it
by yourself. You have to make sure that your heart is
prepared and you know where your eternity lies."

— Sam Aquila

"Jesus said to him, "I am the way, the truth, and the life.
No one comes to the Father except through Me."

— John 14:6

Printed in the USA
CPSIA information can be obtained
at www.ICGtesting.com
LVHW022128300923
759799LV00056B/1272